THE NEW
BELIEVER'S
Friend HANDBOOK

CHARLES CRABTREE
AND
REBECCA GULLION

GPH®
Gospel Publishing House
Springfield, Missouri
02-0280

All scripture quotations, unless otherwise indicated, are taken from the HOLY BIBLE, NEW INTERNATIONAL VERSION®. NIV®. Copyright ©1973, 1978, 1984 by International Bible Society. Used by permission of Zondervan. All rights reserved.

4th Printing 2010

ISBN 978-0882437941

Printed in United States of America

CONTENTS

Helping a new Christian discover biblical truth and begin his or her walk with Christ is a rewarding endeavor.

Not only will you help the new believer start the journey of a lifetime, but through this process you will deepen your own relationship with Christ.

And that's the beauty of discipleship—the mentor is still the student! God bless you and your new friend on your journey together to a more fulfilling relationship with Christ.

WHY DOES A NEW BELIEVER
NEED A CHRISTIAN
FRIEND LIKE YOU?

Imagine you have little or no Christian background, have never been part of an evangelical or Pentecostal church, have little or no Bible knowledge, and have just made the decision to be a believer in Christ. Add to this that you may not have a friend in the new world of church. It's fertile ground for discouragement and frustration.

This is one of the great spiritual tragedies of the church today— the lack of concern and personal attention for babies in Christ. A new believer has just met the greatest Friend the world has ever known and begun an eternal relationship. Angels in heaven rejoice in this fact, and so does the church. But after the celebration comes the challenge of a new life.

In Jesus' Parable of the Lost Son (Luke 15:11–32), the prodigal son found his way back home and enjoyed a great celebration. What happened next? He was probably given new responsibilities and had to adapt again to being at home. He had the benefits of once again living in his father's house (a type of the church) and having friends and family members nearby to help him. In many cases, a new believer doesn't have a church background and may not know how to find help.

A new believer really does need a friend— and that's you!

WHAT IS
THE GOAL
OF BEING A FRIEND
TO A NEW BELIEVER?

The answer to the chapter title question is simple: A good parent wants to see a newborn cared for and nourished until the child can begin to do life's basic tasks without others' help. The same is important spiritually for new believers—care and help are needed until the new believers can do things on their own.

This handbook covers eight weeks of meeting together times for the new believer and friend. After eight weeks, the goals are to see a new believer:

- forging new and wholesome friendships in the church
- entering into the worship service
- attending, comfortable and happy, in a Sunday School class or small group
- beginning to share their faith with family and friends
- forming good spiritual habits, spending time daily in prayer and Bible reading
- choosing to be baptized in water and baptized or seeking to be baptized in the Holy Spirit

Your investment in new believers will give them the needed extra help to survive and flourish as new Christians and will be one of the most satisfying and fulfilling ministries of your life. Thank you for being willing to give of yourself so that other believers can live a healthy Christian life.

WHAT IS YOUR ROLE
AS THE FRIEND OF A
NEW BELIEVER?

The role of a new Christian's friend may feel overwhelming at times. What if you don't know what to say? What if you say the wrong thing?

This chapter focuses on the part you play in the discipleship of the new believer. Here are some general guidelines to help you know what is appropriate and what you should avoid as you assist your new Christian friend.

The following list of dos and don'ts will help you be a better friend to a new believer.

DO

- MAKE A COMMITMENT: Be available and accessible to the new believer for a period of at least eight weeks. Tell the new believer how long you will be their mentor and assure them that you will always be their friend.

- PRAY: Pray for and with the new believer often.

- MEET TOGETHER WEEKLY: Each week the new believer will read one portion from *The New Believer's Handbook*. Set up weekly meetings to go through the week's portion with the new believer. The text of *The New Believer's Handbook* (with study questions and answers) is included in this handbook.

- READ *THE NEW BELIEVER'S HANDBOOK*: Plan to read the weekly portion in preparation for each session with the new believer. A suggested outline for your weekly session is provided, but adapt it by sharing your own insights or to meet the specific needs of the new believer.

- READ THE BOOK OF MARK: The new believer is assigned a portion from the Book of Mark to read daily (two chapters per week). Study questions are included in *The New Believer's Handbook*. Encourage the new believer to set aside time each day for Bible reading and answering the study questions. You should follow the same reading plan during your daily devotions so that you can discuss the Bible reading with the new believer.

- SHARE ANSWERS TO THE STUDY QUESTIONS: The new believer may not be familiar with the Bible. You may need to provide cultural or historical background, spiritual application, or answer any questions for the new believer. To assist you, this handbook includes the answers to the study questions and includes background information for the Bible readings. Adapt to meet the specific needs of the new believer or to share your own insights from the Scripture reading.

- HELP THE NEW BELIEVER GET INVOLVED IN YOUR CHURCH: During the eight-week period, introduce the new believer to people in your church. Offer to go with the new believer to a Sunday School class or a small group. Sit with the new believer in services if possible and if you sense that it would be helpful.

- HELP THE NEW BELIEVER TAKE INITIAL STEPS: As the new believer grows as a Christian, emphasize the need to obey Bible instructions for water and Spirit baptism. Encourage the new believer to attend church services regularly.

- HELP THE NEW BELIEVER ESTABLISH GOOD HABITS: Lead the new believer in establishing the spiritual disciplines of daily prayer, Bible study, and personal devotions. Consider making *God's Word for Today* (a daily devotional) available to them online at www.ag.org/top/devotional or as a subscription from Gospel Publishing House at www.GospelPublishing.com.

- INVOLVE YOUR PASTOR: Report to the pastor (or designated leader) from time to time on the progress of the new believer and seek the pastor's counsel if needed.

- JUST BE A FRIEND! Love never fails. Love helps first-time parents do the right things without much training. The same will hold true for you as you mentor the new believer.

DON'T

- SMOTHER OR OVERWHELM THE NEW BELIEVER: Do as much or as little as needed by following their lead and sensing the guidance of the Holy Spirit.

- DEMAND: Simply offer and appeal. Many new believers are very sensitive and fearful. The last thing they need is stern correction or a task master.

- TRY TO BE A PSYCHOLOGIST: Encourage the new believer to get help through the pastor or pastoral staff for problems beyond your expertise. Remember, you are their friend—not a doctor, banker, or theologian.

- BE CRITICAL OF ANYONE OR ANYTHING IN THE CHURCH: It's not your job to point out flaws or imperfections in other believers; your job is to hold up the perfection of Jesus. If the new believer is critical, use it as a learning moment to explain how to leave such things in God's hands.

- BE RESPONSIBLE FOR THEM: You are responsible to the new believer, not for them. Remember when you have done your best, how they respond to truth and counsel is not your responsibility.

WHAT HAPPENED TO ME?

BEFORE YOU MEET

☐ Schedule a time to meet with the new believer.

☐ Read Week 1 of *The New Believer's Handbook*.

☐ Read the Week 1 Bible readings from Mark.

☐ Review the study questions.

☐ Prepare to share your testimony with the new believer (see Share Together section).

☐ Use a Bible in a modern translation. Make sure the new believer has one too.

MEET TOGETHER

▶ Greet the new believer.

▶ Pray together that God will guide your time of study and fellowship.

REVIEW TOGETHER

▶ Answer the new believer's questions about the Introduction and the Week 1 reading.

▶ Highlight the following from Week 1 in *The New Believer's Handbook* and supporting information:

Understanding Salvation

- New life: You are born again spiritually.
- New chance: The new life means that past sins are gone and guilt is removed.
- New boss: Every believer has a new boss—Jesus is Lord of your life.

► Review Week 1 Bible readings and study questions from Mark. Ask if the new believer has any questions. (See Bible Background Information [page 130] for additional helps if needed.)

SHARE TOGETHER

► Share your testimony and include the following:
- "How I became a Christian"
- "How I felt after I became a Christian"
- "What I did the first week as a new believer"
- "God's Word, the Bible, has helped me . . ."

► Ask the new believer these questions:
- [?] What does being saved mean to you?
- [?] Did you tell your family and friends about your salvation? What did you say?
- [?] What kind of changes do you think are coming because of your commitment to Jesus Christ?

PRAY TOGETHER

► Ask the new believer for any prayer requests.

► Pray together.

WRAPPING UP

► Schedule your next meeting with the new believer.

► Remind the new believer to:
- Read Week 2 of *The New Believer's Handbook*,
- Read the Week 2 Bible readings from Mark, and
- Complete the study questions.

CONGRATULATIONS!

You just made the best decision of your life by accepting Jesus as your Lord and Savior. But what happens now? Where do you go from here?

The upcoming weeks are key as you begin a new life as a Christian, or follower of Jesus Christ and His teachings. Just like anything new, there will be some clear differences from the old. This handbook will help you understand those differences and get you started in the right direction. It gives guidance for the next eight weeks, with a chapter designed for each. Read the chapters carefully, and follow the helps given.

One of the first things to do in this new life is obtain a Bible and read some of it every day. The Bible is God's written message to all people. It helps us better understand who God is and how to make Him part of our lives. Use a Bible written in a modern translation, such as the New International Version, *New Living Translation*, or New King James Version. Bibles can be purchased at a book or discount store.

You should also find a good Christian friend to help guide you in your new life. This friend can help you answer the questions you will have along the way, and offer support when you need it. This Christian friend can also help you choose a good Bible translation.

Each chapter of this handbook includes some basic teaching about being a Christian, a daily Bible reading plan, and Bible study questions. The Bible reading plan will walk you through a short portion of the Bible named after its writer, Mark. It is found about two-thirds of the way through the Bible in a section called the New Testament. Mark recounts the good news about the life of Jesus Christ.

The Bible study questions at the end of each day's reading will take very little time, and they will help you understand how to effectively study the Bible. The total time needed for the Bible study each day is less than half an hour.

Do your best and God will help you!

WEEK 1

WHAT HAPPENED TO ME?

Just what has happened to you exactly?
That's a good question, and an important one.
Knowing what happened and what it means will
help you best begin your new life as a Christian.

It may have happened in a church, in your home,
anywhere. Someone may have been with you,
or perhaps you were by yourself. Maybe you felt
something missing in your life, or you turned to
Jesus for help in a desperate situation. One way
or another, you asked Him to be a part of your life.

Now, what does it all mean? To put it
simply, two things have happened:

1. Jesus has become your Savior.

2. You have become a child of God.

We call this salvation. Perhaps someone
has already said that now you are saved. Maybe
you wonder what that means. Saved from what?
Why did you need to be saved? Three things are
important for you to know:

1. You were a sinner.

2. You could not save yourself.

3. Only Jesus could save you.

The Bible says, "All have sinned" (Romans 3:23).
Sin is doing anything that you know is wrong, and
everyone, except Jesus, has done this. The Bible

also says, "The wages of sin is death" (Romans 6:23). This kind of death is spiritual and eternal.

No one can be saved from this death by good works, church membership, or trying to be a moral person. The only way to be saved from the penalty of sin is to somehow provide payment.

Jesus provided the only sufficient payment for sin by dying on a cross many years ago. He took upon himself the punishment for all sin. When you asked God to forgive your sins and believed Jesus died for you, God accepted you for Jesus' sake, your sins were forgiven, and Jesus became your Savior.

But something else has happened. You have become a child of God.

A child of God? What does that mean? Look at it this way. When you were born as a baby, you received natural life from your parents. Because of this, you are like them and have many of their characteristics.

When Jesus became your Savior, He brought you new life, spiritual life, life from God. The Bible calls this the new birth (John 3:3). By your first birth, you became a child of your earthly parents; by your new birth, you have become a child of God.

This is important! You now have two natures: (1) the old nature you received when physically born the first time and (2) the new nature you received with the new, spiritual birth. Jesus Christ is now living with you by His Holy Spirit. The Holy Spirit is God, living inside Christians, giving them power to live like Jesus. You are living a new life with a new nature that draws you away from sin and to Jesus.

As far as your first, or natural, birth is concerned, you may be an adult, a youth, or a child. But as far as your new, or spiritual, birth is concerned, you are a newborn. You have received a new life, but it's just beginning.

During these next few weeks your new nature will begin to grow stronger as you develop good habits. These are very important weeks as you set the patterns to base the rest of your life on.

Next is your Bible reading plan and study questions for this first week. These will help you develop a habit of reading and studying the Bible.

WEEK ONE ▪ DAY ONE
Bible Reading & Study Questions from Mark 1:1–8

1. What did the prophet Isaiah say John would do? (Mark 1:2,3) *Prepare the way for the Lord*

2. What two things did John do to prepare the way for Jesus? (Mark 1:4) *Baptize and preach*

3. What kind of baptism did John preach and perform? (Mark 1:4) *Baptism of repentance for the forgiveness of sins*

4. What did John say Jesus would baptize with? (Mark 1:8) *The Holy Spirit*

WEEK ONE ▪ DAY TWO
Bible Reading & Study Questions from Mark 1:9–20

1. What was the role of the Holy Spirit at Jesus' water baptism? (Mark 1:10) *The Holy Spirit descended on Jesus like a dove.*

2. What was God's response to Jesus' water baptism? (Mark 1:11) *God said, "You are my Son, whom I love; with you I am well pleased."*

3. What did Jesus say a person should do to prepare for the kingdom of God? (Mark 1:15) *Repent and believe the good news*

4. What did Jesus tell Simon and Andrew He would make them? (Mark 1:17) **Fishers of men**

WEEK ONE ▪ DAY THREE
Bible Reading & Study Questions from Mark 1:21–34

1. Why were the people amazed at Jesus' teaching? (Mark 1:22) **Because He taught them as one who had authority, not as the teachers of the law**

2. What did the evil spirit know about Jesus? (Mark 1:24) **That He was the Holy One of God**

3. What did Simon's mother-in-law do after Jesus healed her? (Mark 1:31) **She waited on Him.**

4. Who did the people bring to Jesus to be healed? (Mark 1:32) **All the sick and demon possessed**

WEEK ONE ▪ DAY FOUR
Bible Reading & Study Questions from Mark 1:35–45

1. What time of day did Jesus pray? (Mark 1:35) **Early in the morning**

2. When the man with leprosy asked if Jesus was willing to heal him, what did Jesus say? (Mark 1:41) **"I am willing. Be clean."**

3. What did the man with leprosy do after Jesus healed him? (Mark 1:45) **He spread the news about Jesus.**

WEEK ONE ▪ DAY FIVE
Bible Reading & Study Questions from Mark 2:1–12

1. Whose faith did Jesus respond to in healing the paralytic man? (Mark 2:5) **The friends of the paralytic man**

2. What did Jesus say to the paralytic man? (Mark 2:5) **"Son, your sins are forgiven."**

3. Why did Jesus' statement to the paralytic man upset the teachers of the Law? (Mark 2:6) **Only God can forgive sins.**

4. What did healing the paralytic man prove? (Mark 2:10) **That Jesus has the power to forgive sins**

5. If only God can forgive sins (Mark 2:6) but Jesus also has the power to forgive sins (Mark 2:10), what do these verses tell us about Jesus? **Jesus is God.**

WEEK ONE ▪ DAY SIX
Bible Reading & Study Questions from Mark 2:13–22

1. Who did Jesus spend time with? (Mark 2:15) *Tax collectors and sinners*

2. Who did Jesus compare sinners to? (Mark 2:17) *The sick*

3. Who did Jesus compare himself to? (Mark 2:17) *A doctor*

4. Who else did Jesus compare himself to? (Mark 2:19) *A bridegroom*

WEEK ONE ▪ DAY SEVEN
Bible Reading & Study Questions from Mark 2:23–28

1. What were Jesus' disciples doing on the Sabbath? (Mark 2:23) *Picking grain*

2. What person did Jesus use as an example to justify His disciples' actions? (Mark 2:25) *David*

3. What did Jesus say to defend His disciples? (Mark 2:27) *"The Sabbath was made for man, not man for the Sabbath."*

4. Who is Lord of the Sabbath? (Mark 2:28) *The Son of Man (Jesus)*

WHERE DO I GO FROM HERE?

BEFORE YOU MEET

- ☐ Schedule a time to meet with the new believer.
- ☐ Read Week 2 of *The New Believer's Handbook*.
- ☐ Read the Week 2 Bible readings from Mark.
- ☐ Review the study questions.
- ☐ Prepare to share with the new believer about your witnessing experiences (good and bad) and your learning to be obedient to God's Word.
- ☐ Prepare to discuss how to make time for basic spiritual disciplines (Bible reading, prayer, church attendance).

MEET TOGETHER

▶ Greet the new believer.

▶ Pray together that God will guide your time of study and fellowship.

REVIEW TOGETHER

▶ Answer the new believer's questions about the Week 2 reading.

▶ Highlight the following from Week 2 in *The New Believer's Handbook* and supporting information:

Spiritual Life
- Jesus is the Source of spiritual life.

Spiritual Growth
- Spiritual growth follows the pattern of normal physical growth: baby first, child, youth, moving to maturity.

Growth goals for new Christians are to be:
- Strong
- Healthy
- Mature
- Disciplined

Spiritual Food
- To grow, believers need spiritual food.

Results of a balanced diet:
- Growth
- Life

Results of an unbalanced diet:
- Stunted growth
- Ultimately death

Necessary spiritual food:
- Read the Bible
- Pray
- Witness to others
- Attend church regularly
- Be obedient

▶ Review Week 2 Bible readings and study questions from Mark. Ask if the new believer has any questions. (See Bible Background Information [page 133] for additional helps if needed.)

·········· SHARE TOGETHER

▶ Describe ways believers can make time to
- Read the Bible daily
- Pray daily
- Attend church services regularly

► Share with the new believer your experiences in witnessing and learning to be obedient.

► Ask the new believer these questions:

　? What are the difficulties in setting aside time every day to read the Bible?

　? How has your desire for reading the Bible grown?

　? What choices did you face this week in which you asked, "Will this be pleasing to God?" because of your commitment to Jesus Christ?

PRAY TOGETHER

► Ask the new believer for any prayer requests.

► Pray together.

WRAPPING UP

► Schedule your next meeting with the new believer.

► Remind the new believer to:

- Read Week 3 of *The New Believer's Handbook*,
- Read the Week 3 Bible readings from Mark, and
- Complete the study questions.

WEEK 2

WHERE DO I GO FROM HERE?

Week 1 established that you're a spiritual newborn, with need of maturity. So where do you go from here?

It is tragic when, because of a physical affliction, a child fails to mature and mentally remains a baby for life. It's even more tragic when a person becomes a child of God through salvation and then fails to mature spiritually.

This doesn't have to happen to you. As you follow these suggestions, you can begin to become a strong, mature Christian.

First of all, remember that your spiritual life comes from Jesus, the Son of God. "God has given us eternal life, and this life is in his Son. He who has the Son has life; he who does not have the Son of God does not have life" (1 John 5:11,12).

Receiving life is not enough; you must nourish that life. When a baby is born in the natural, it will die unless its parents (or someone) take care of it. They must feed and nourish the baby's physical life so it will grow.

This is also true in relation to your new spiritual life. If you feed it, it will grow; if you neglect it, it will die. "Like newborn babies, crave pure spiritual milk, so that by it you may grow up in your salvation" (1 Peter 2:2).

It's as simple as that. Your spiritual growth depends on how and what you feed yourself spiritually. Here are some keys that will help you grow.

READ THE BIBLE

In week 3 we'll talk more about the Bible. Your use of the Bible will determine the kind of Christian you will be. This is why we've provided a Bible reading plan for your first few weeks. Make a habit of reading the Bible every day.

PRAY

In week 4 we'll talk about various kinds of prayer and how to pray effectively. The simplest way to describe prayer is that it is talking to God and letting Him talk to us. Make time every day to pray.

For many people, the best time to pray is the first thing in the morning, before starting daily activities. Talk to Him as you would to a friend— He is your best Friend and you can talk to Him anytime. Don't worry about using the right words. God is more concerned with your attitude than with your vocabulary.

WITNESS TO OTHERS

Tell others about what has happened to you.
A witness is someone who tells others about
something he or she has learned personally. If you
have learned that Jesus can forgive, let others
know about it too.

Witnessing is saying and doing things that
point people to Jesus. Let everyone know how
wonderful your new Friend can be to him or her.
Witnessing will make you a stronger Christian.

ATTEND CHURCH REGULARLY

If you take a live coal from the fireplace and put
it by itself, it will soon go out. But, it can keep its
heat and even ignite other materials if it is kept in
the fireplace near other coals.

In the same way, Christians need the
encouragement of other Christians, which comes
by attending church. Listening to the pastor
and other mature Christians preach and teach
the Word of God, praying with others, singing
together, making Christian friendships—these will
help you grow (Hebrews 10:25).

BE OBEDIENT

When God asks you to do or not to do something,
obey quickly. Jesus is your Master as well as

your Savior. Here is a good question to ask when deciding what is right or wrong: Will this be pleasing to God? Make this the ruling factor in all you do or say.

Spiritual maturity does not depend on how long you have been saved. It depends on how committed you are to doing what it takes to become spiritually mature.

WEEK TWO ▪ DAY ONE
Bible Reading & Study Questions from Mark 3:1–19

1. What did Jesus ask the Pharisees to help them understand the intent of the Sabbath? (Mark 3:4) ***"Which is lawful on the Sabbath: to do good or to do evil, to save life or to kill?"***

2. What was the Pharisees' problem? (Mark 3:5) ***They had stubborn hearts.***

3. Who did the evil spirits recognize Jesus to be? (Mark 3:11) ***The Son of God***

4. What three duties are mentioned for the twelve apostles? (Mark 3:14) ***Be with Jesus, preach, and drive out demons***

WEEK TWO • DAY TWO
Bible Reading & Study Questions from Mark 3:20–35

1. What did the teachers of the law accuse Jesus of? (Mark 3:22,30) *Being possessed by an evil spirit, and driving out spirits by the power of the prince of demons (Satan)*

2. What three reasons would prevent Satan from opposing himself? (Mark 3:26) *He would be divided, he could not stand, and his end would come.*

3. What sins can be forgiven? (Mark 3:28) *All sins against man*

4. Who is a part of Jesus' family? (Mark 3:35) *Whoever does God's will*

WEEK TWO • DAY THREE
Bible Reading & Study Questions from Mark 4:1–20

1. What does the "seed" represent? (Mark 4:14) *God's Word*

2. What happens to the "seed" that falls along the path? (Mark 4:15) *Satan comes and takes it away.*

3. Why do people who are on "rocky ground" turn away from God quickly? (Mark 4:17) **They have no root.**

4. What prevents people who are on "thorny ground" from producing fruit? (Mark 4:19) **The worries of this life, the deceitfulness of wealth, and the desires for other things come in and choke the Word.**

5. What type of crop do people who are on "good ground" produce? (Mark 4:20) **Thirty, sixty, or even a hundred times what was sown**

WEEK TWO ▪ DAY FOUR
Bible Reading & Study Questions from Mark 4:21–25

1. Where do you put a lamp? (Mark 4:21) **On a stand**

2. Psalm 119:11 indicates we should hide God's Word (the Bible) in our hearts. What does Mark say we should do with God's hidden Word? (Mark 4:22) **Disclose it; bring it out into the open**

3. What two things should we do after hearing the Word of God? (Mark 4:24) **Carefully consider it and use it.**

WEEK TWO • DAY FIVE
Bible Reading & Study Questions from Mark 4:26–29

1. What happens to the seed after it is scattered?
(Mark 4:27) *It sprouts and grows.*

2. What is produced? (Mark 4:28) *Grain*

3. What happens after the grain is ripe? (Mark 4:29)
It is harvested.

WEEK TWO • DAY SIX
Bible Reading & Study Questions from Mark 4:30–34

1. What small seed does Jesus use as an
illustration? (Mark 4:31) *Mustard seed*

2. What happens after the seed is planted?
(Mark 4:32) *It grows to be very large.*

3. What did Jesus use to teach the crowds?
(Mark 4:33,34) *Parables*

4. What did Jesus do differently with His disciples?
(Mark 4:34) *He explained everything to them.*

WEEK TWO · DAY SEVEN
Bible Reading & Study Questions from Mark 4:35–41

1. What was Jesus doing while on the boat when
   the storm arose? (Mark 4:38) *Sleeping*

2. What did Jesus' disciples ask Him? (Mark 4:38)
   "Teacher, don't you care if we drown?"

3. How did Jesus show His disciples that He cared
   what happened to them? (Mark 4:39) *He calmed
   the sea.*

4. What did the disciples' fear of the storm
   indicate? (Mark 4:40) *Lack of faith*

HOW CAN I UNDERSTAND THE BIBLE?

BEFORE YOU MEET

- ☐ Schedule a time to meet with the new believer.
- ☐ Read Week 3 of *The New Believer's Handbook*.
- ☐ Read the Week 3 Bible readings from Mark.
- ☐ Review the study questions.
- ☐ Prepare to share tips with the new believer for Scripture memorization and Bible study and comprehension (see Share Together section).
- ☐ Read 2 Timothy 3:14–17. Use the six categories of questions in *The New Believer's Handbook* to help you complete your study of the passage. Write out your responses to share with the new believer.

MEET TOGETHER

▶ Greet the new believer.

▶ Pray together that God will guide your time of study and fellowship.

REVIEW TOGETHER

▶ Answer the new believer's questions about the Week 3 reading.

▶ Highlight the following from Week 3 in *The New Believer's Handbook* and supporting information:

How to make the Bible part of your life:
- ▪ Read the Word
- ▪ Hear the Word

- Study the Word
  - **Intent:** What does this verse say and how does it apply to me?
  - **Difficulty:** What does this verse say that I don't understand?
  - **Comparison:** What similar thoughts are found elsewhere in the Bible?
  - **Promises:** What blessings are stated and are they for all people including me?
  - **Warnings:** What warnings should I pay attention to?
  - **Commands:** What commands should I obey?
- Memorize the Word
- Meditate on the Word

▶ Review Week 3 Bible readings and study questions from Mark. Ask if the new believer has any questions. (See Bible Background Information [page 134] for additional helps if needed.)

········· SHARE TOGETHER

▶ Describe the methods you use for Scripture memorization and Bible study and comprehension.

▶ Use 2 Timothy 3:14–17 to practice using the six categories of questions on how to study the Bible.

▶ Ask the new believer these questions:
  - ? How has reading the Book of Mark helped you?
  - ? Which Bible passages have been difficult to understand?
  - ? What have been the results of asking God to help you understand and apply what you are reading?
  - ? How have you benefited from meditating on the Bible verses, thinking about them throughout your day?

PRAY TOGETHER

▶ Ask the new believer for any prayer requests.

▶ Pray together.

WRAPPING UP

▶ Schedule your next meeting with the new believer.

▶ Remind the new believer to:
- Read Week 4 of *The New Believer's Handbook*,
- Read the Week 4 Bible readings from Mark, and
- Complete the study questions.

WEEK 3

HOW CAN I UNDERSTAND THE BIBLE?

As mentioned in week 2, reading the Bible is one of the best ways to be fed and help your spiritual growth. It is "able to make you wise for salvation through faith in Christ Jesus. All Scripture is God-breathed and is useful for teaching, rebuking, correcting and training in righteousness, so that the man of God may be thoroughly equipped for every good work" (2 Timothy 3:15–17).

The Bible is often called *the Word* because it is one of God's ways of communicating with us. We use words to express ourselves to others. God uses the Bible to express himself to us. There are five common ways to make the Bible a part of your life.

READ THE WORD

Habits influence our character, and one of the best habits you can have to form good character is to read the Bible every day. The best way to make Bible reading a habit is to establish a regular time and place to do your reading. Repetition and familiarity create habits.

Set a reasonable pace for yourself. Start by reading fifteen minutes a day. Many people find the best time of day is in the morning. Other possible reading times include before going to bed at night or during lunchtime. It's not really important what time of day you choose; it is important that you set aside time in your schedule to read the Bible each day without distractions.

We suggest using a Bible in a modern translation, such as the New International Version, *New Living Translation*, or New King James Version. Use a Bible in which you can underline with a pen and write notes in the margin. See page 80 for suggestions about what to read after you finish reading the Book of Mark.

HEAR THE WORD

Because hearing is another way of receiving the Word of God into your life, it is important that you form the habit of attending church services as often as possible. There you will hear the pastor and other mature Christians preach and teach the Word of God. Taking notes will help you remember what you hear.

STUDY THE WORD

Studying the Bible takes time, but is an extremely valuable exercise for understanding it. For in-depth studying you will need longer time periods, usually an hour at least—perhaps an entire evening when you have a free one.

The Bible is one method God uses to communicate to you. Parts of the Bible can seem unclear and need more study to understand them better. When a passage is unclear, pray and ask God to help you concentrate on, understand, and apply what you are reading. Then try re-reading the passage. If you still have problems, write down the questions so you can ask another Christian.

When you are studying a passage, use the following categorized questions to help you better understand what you are reading.

Intent. What does this passage or verse say? What did the writer mean when it was originally written? Who was it written to? What are the subjects it addresses? How does it apply to you?

Difficulty. What does this verse or passage say that you don't understand? What particular words or phrases make it unclear?

Comparison. What similar thoughts are found elsewhere in the Bible? (The more you study, the more you see common threads throughout the Bible.)

Promises. What blessings and helps are stated or implied? Were they intended for a specific individual or for all people?

Warnings. What warnings do you find? How do these warnings apply to your everyday life?

Commands. What commands are stated or implied for you to obey?

MEMORIZE THE WORD

Memorization of verses is another way to help you use God's Word in your daily life. Also, it is one way to obey the verse, "I have hidden your word in my heart that I might not sin against you" (Psalm 119:11).

Start with some of the verses listed at the end of this handbook. Look at the various parts of the verse you are memorizing to see what each means. Then, notice the important words. For example, in Psalm 119:11 the important words are *hidden*, *word*, and *heart*. Focusing on the important words of the verse will help you memorize it. Memorize the reference as well so you can help others find it.

MEDITATE ON THE WORD

After you have read, heard, studied, and memorized a Bible verse, you have something to meditate (intently think) on. In the spare moments of the day—working around the house, waiting for an elevator, driving down the street—you can clear your mind and meditate on Bible verses you have learned. If you can't sleep at night, try thinking about a verse or passage from the Bible.

WEEK THREE • DAY ONE
Bible Reading & Study Questions from Mark 5:1–20

1. List the four things that describe the man with an evil spirit prior to his meeting Jesus.
(Mark 5:3–5) *He lived in the tombs; no one could subdue him; he cried out; he cut himself with stones.*

2. List the three actions of the demon-possessed man after his encounter with Jesus. (Mark 5:15) *He was sitting, dressed, and in his right mind.*

3. What did Jesus tell the man to do? (Mark 5:19) *"Go home to your family and tell them how much the Lord has done for you, and how he has had mercy on you."*

WEEK THREE ▪ DAY TWO
Bible Reading & Study Questions from Mark 5:21–43

1. How long had the woman been subject to bleeding? (Mark 5:25) **Twelve years**

2. What happened immediately after she touched Jesus' clothing? (Mark 5:29) **The bleeding stopped.**

3. How did Jesus know that someone in the large crowd had touched His clothes? (Mark 5:30) **He felt power go out of Him.**

4. What did Jesus tell the woman? (Mark 5:34) **"Daughter, your faith has healed you. Go in peace and be freed from your suffering."**

5. What happened to Jairus's sick daughter before Jesus could arrive? (Mark 5:35) **She died.**

6. What did Jesus do? (Mark 5:40–43) **He brought her back to life.**

7. How old was Jairus's daughter? (Mark 5:42) **Twelve years old**

WEEK THREE ▪ DAY THREE
Bible Reading & Study Questions from Mark 6:1–6

1. Why were the people in Jesus' hometown amazed about Him? (Mark 6:2) *Because of His wisdom and miracles*

2. Why were they offended? (Mark 6:3) *Because they knew where He came from and who His family was*

3. What amazed Jesus and why couldn't He do many miracles there? (Mark 6:6) *The people's lack of faith*

WEEK THREE ▪ DAY FOUR
Bible Reading & Study Questions from Mark 6:7–13

1. What did Jesus give the Twelve authority over? (Mark 6:7) *Evil spirits*

2. How do we know that Jesus wanted the Twelve to be cared for by the people they ministered to? (Mark 6:8–10) *He told them not to take food or money for their journey, not to bother with an extra change of clothes, and to stay in people's homes.*

3. What did the Twelve preach? (Mark 6:12) *That people should repent*

WEEK THREE ▪ DAY FIVE
Bible Reading & Study Questions from Mark 6:14–29

1. Why did Herod's wife, Herodias, hold a grudge against John the Baptist? (Mark 6:18) **John had said it was unlawful for Herod to be married to her, since she was his brother's wife.**

2. Why did Herod not want to kill John? (Mark 6:20) **Herod feared him because John was a righteous and holy man.**

3. Why did Herod kill John? (Mark 6:26) **Herod had given an oath and his dinner guests had heard him say it.**

4. How was John executed? (Mark 6:27,28) **He was beheaded.**

WEEK THREE ▪ DAY SIX
Bible Reading & Study Questions from Mark 6:30–44

1. Why did Jesus have compassion on the crowd? (Mark 6:34) **They were like sheep without a shepherd.**

2. Name two ways Jesus showed compassion on the crowd. (Mark 6:34,41–42) **He taught them and He fed them.**

3. How many loaves and fish did Jesus give thanks for? How much food was left over? (Mark 6:38,43) *Five loaves and two fish; twelve baskets*

4. How many men were fed? (Mark 6:44) *Five thousand*

WEEK THREE ▪ DAY SEVEN
Bible Reading & Study Questions from Mark 6:45–56

1. What did Jesus do following the feeding of the five thousand? (Mark 6:45,46) *He sent His disciples ahead of Him, by boat, to the next town; He dismissed the crowds; and He went to the mountainside to pray.*

2. What did Jesus do when He saw that the disciples were having difficulty rowing the boat because of the strong wind? (Mark 6:48) *He went out to them, walking on the lake.*

3. What happened as soon as Jesus climbed into the boat? (Mark 6:51) *The wind died down.*

HOW CAN I PRAY EFFECTIVELY?

BEFORE YOU MEET

- [ ] Schedule a time to meet with the new believer.
- [ ] Read Week 4 of *The New Believer's Handbook*.
- [ ] Read the Week 4 Bible readings from Mark.
- [ ] Review the study questions.
- [ ] Create a list of tips for making time in the day for consistent prayer. Include ways you have made time in your daily life for prayer.
- [ ] Think of times that God has spoken to you. Be prepared to share your testimony with the new believer (see Share Together section).

MEET TOGETHER

▶ Greet the new believer.

▶ Ask the new believer to lead in your prayer together that God will guide your time of study and fellowship. If the new believer isn't ready to pray aloud, don't make it an issue. Explain that praying aloud will become easier as the new believer becomes more comfortable praying.

REVIEW TOGETHER

▶ Answer the new believer's questions about the Week 4 reading.

▶ Highlight the following from Week 4 in *The New Believer's Handbook* and supporting information:

If Bible reading is spiritual nourishment, then prayer can be compared to breathing.

Two facets of prayer:

- Talking to God (exhaling)
  - Praise
  - Thanksgiving
  - Repentance
  - Petition
  - Intercession
- Listening to God (inhaling)
  - Answers
    - Yes
    - No
    - Wait
  - How God speaks to us
    - God can speak in an audible voice (rare even in Bible).
    - God speaks to our heart. We have a strong impression about what step we are to take or not to take. This direction will align with the Bible if it is from God.
    - God speaks through the Bible.
    - God speaks through other Christians. Again, this direction should agree with what the Bible says.

What to pray about:
- Your needs
- Needs of others

▶ Review Week 4 Bible readings and study questions from Mark. Ask if the new believer has any questions. (See Bible Background Information [page 135] for additional helps if needed.)

SHARE TOGETHER

▶ Discuss tips for making time in the day for consistent times of prayer.

▶ It is not possible to find time for prayer; each person must make time in the day for prayer.

▶ Possible places to find time:
- While driving or commuting to work
- During exercise
- Waking up earlier or staying up later
- Giving up a TV show or other hobby time

▶ Share with the new believer experiences of God speaking to you.

▶ Ask the new believer these questions:
- ? How has prayer helped you?
- ? What struggles are you having in prayer?
- ? How has God spoken to you?

PRAY TOGETHER

▶ Ask the new believer for any prayer requests.

▶ Pray together.

WRAPPING UP

▶ Schedule your next meeting with the new believer.

▶ Remind the new believer to:
- Read Week 5 of *The New Believer's Handbook*,
- Read the Week 5 Bible readings from Mark, and
- Complete the study questions.

HOW CAN I PRAY EFFECTIVELY?

If the Bible can be compared to food because it nourishes our spiritual lives, then prayer can be compared to breathing. There are two parts to breathing—inhaling and exhaling. So it is with prayer—talking to God and listening for His response.

The person who says, "I can't find time for prayer," may have a point. Most people have to make time for prayer. A good time to pray regularly is along with your Bible reading. In fact, when something you read stands out, stop for a few moments and pray about it.

One trait of a solid, mature Christian is a consistent prayer life.

WHAT TO PRAY ABOUT

One of your first challenges when learning to pray is knowing what to pray about. Most people think of their family, friends, associates, and personal needs—then in five minutes they have run out of things to say. One way to solve this problem is to focus your prayer on certain topics, a different topic each day. Page 83 of this handbook has suggestions. Another solution is to utilize different kinds of prayer.

KINDS OF PRAYER

Prayer is simply talking to God, but there are several ways you can do it. The following kinds of prayer will bring variety into your conversations with God.

Praise. In praise you speak highly to God about who He is and His greatness. The focus of praise is the personhood of God. One way you can do this is by reading or quoting verses from the Book of Psalms like, "The Lord is gracious and righteous; our God is full of compassion" (Psalm 116:5).

Thanksgiving. Prayer also includes thanking God for what He has done for you and others. In fact, thanksgiving is a good way to begin your prayers. It builds your faith in what God can do for you by remembering what He has already done.

Repentance. In repentance, you admit your wrongs to God, ask for His forgiveness, and commit to turn away from sin and live the way He wants you to. Because no one is perfect and everyone makes mistakes, repentance helps us mend our relationship with God when we fail.

Petition. This means asking God to meet certain needs. Though some people never progress beyond the "gimme" stage of their prayer life, always asking God for something, there is nothing wrong with asking the Lord for His help when you need it. In fact, God strongly encourages us to come to Him with our needs.

Intercession. Sometimes you may feel the need to pray for someone else until you have the assurance that God has answered your prayer. This is intercession, one of the greatest kinds of prayer. In intercession your prayers are focused on others and their needs, rather than your own. This kind of prayer is vital for the Christian community.

Take a few moments to carefully read the Lord's Prayer in Matthew 6:9–13. See if you can identify the different kinds of prayer in this model prayer that Jesus taught His disciples.

HOW GOD ANSWERS

This is an important lesson to learn: God answers every prayer. Sometimes He says, "Yes," sometimes He says, "No," and often He says, "Wait." But time spent in prayer is never wasted. Even more than what He does *for* you, God is interested in what He can do *in* you. Prayer changes you.

PRAYING IN PUBLIC

Sooner or later, someone will ask you to lead in prayer. Don't panic. Simply remember that you're

praying to the Lord, not to the people. Pray as
a representative of the group and express what
you think are the general desires in that meeting.
Don't worry about using fancy words; just be
honest, clear, and precise.

WEEK FOUR ▪ DAY ONE
Bible Reading & Study Questions from Mark 7:1–23

1. What were the Pharisees holding on to?
   (Mark 7:8) **The traditions of men**

2. What was the problem with the Pharisees'
   observance of traditions? (Mark 7:13) **They were
   nullifying, canceling out, the Word of God.**

3. What things that come from within make a
   person "unclean"? (Mark 7:21,22) **Evil thoughts,
   sexual immorality, theft, murder, adultery,
   greed, malice, deceit, lewdness, envy, slander,
   arrogance, and folly**

WEEK FOUR ▪ DAY TWO
Bible Reading & Study Questions from Mark 7:24–30

1. What nationality was the woman and where
   was she from? (Mark 7:26) **Greek, born in Syrian
   Phoenicia**

2. What did the woman want Jesus to do?
   (Mark 7:26) **Drive the demon out of her
   daughter**

3. What did Jesus do after the woman replied to His remark? (Mark 7:29) *He healed her daughter (made the demon leave the girl).*

WEEK FOUR ▪ DAY THREE
Bible Reading & Study Questions from Mark 7:31–37

1. Describe the method Jesus used to heal the deaf and mute man. (Mark 7:33) *Jesus took him aside, away from the crowd, put His fingers into the man's ears, then spit and touched the man's tongue.*

2. What words did Jesus use when healing the man? (Mark 7:34) *Be opened!*

3. What was the people's reaction after hearing about the healing? (Mark 7:37) *They were overwhelmed with amazement.*

WEEK FOUR ▪ DAY FOUR
Bible Reading & Study Questions from Mark 8:1–13

1. What was Jesus' attitude toward the crowd who had followed Him for three days without food? (Mark 8:2) *He had compassion on them.*

2. How many loaves of bread and fish did Jesus use to feed the crowd? (Mark 8:5,7) *Seven loaves of bread and a few fish*

3. How many basketfuls of food were left over after everyone ate and was satisfied? (Mark 8:8) *Seven*

4. How many men, besides women and children, were fed? (Mark 8:9) *Four thousand men*

5. After the miraculous feeding of the four thousand, what did the Pharisees ask Jesus for to test Him? (Mark 8:11) *A sign from heaven*

WEEK FOUR ▪ DAY FIVE
Bible Reading & Study Questions from Mark 8:14–21

1. Why did the disciples think Jesus was warning them about the yeast (teaching) of the Pharisees? (Mark 8:14,16) *Because they'd forgotten to bring extra bread with them*

2. What two miracles did Jesus use as examples to show the disciples they had misunderstood His warning? (Mark 8:19,20) *Feeding of the five thousand and the four thousand*

WEEK FOUR ▪ DAY SIX
Bible Reading & Study Questions from Mark 8:22–26

1. Describe the method Jesus used to heal the blind man. (Mark 8:23,25) *Jesus took him by the hand and led him outside the village, spit on his eyes, and put His hands on the man's eyes.*

2. Rather than the healing being immediate, what was the first result? (Mark 8:24) *The man saw people that looked like trees.*

WEEK FOUR ▪ DAY SEVEN
Bible Reading & Study Questions from Mark 8:27–38

1. Who did Peter say Jesus was? (Mark 8:29) *The Christ*

2. Jesus told His followers that He must suffer, be rejected, and then be killed. What three things did Jesus say a person must do to be His follower? (Mark 8:34) *Deny himself, take up his cross, and follow Jesus.*

3. What did Jesus teach would happen to the people who lose their lives for Him and the gospel? (Mark 8:35) *They would save their life.*

4. What did Jesus say is worth more than all the world? (Mark 8:36) *A person's soul*

HOW CAN I BE A STRONG CHRISTIAN?

BEFORE YOU MEET

☐ Schedule a time to meet with the new believer.

☐ Read Week 5 of *The New Believer's Handbook*.

☐ Read the Week 5 Bible readings from Mark.

☐ Review the study questions.

☐ Think of specific examples in your life when you have overcome temptation (see Share Together section).

☐ Prepare to share with the new believer examples of things you struggle with and how God has helped you overcome them. Include about your struggles with disappointment.

MEET TOGETHER

▶ Greet the new believer.

▶ Pray together that God will guide your time of study and fellowship.

REVIEW TOGETHER

▶ Answer the new believer's questions about the Week 5 reading.

▶ Highlight the following from Week 5 in *The New Believer's Handbook* and supporting information.

Power to Overcome
- Recognize and resist temptation
- Know your weak points
- Cooperate with God
- Focus on God's Word
- Avoid discouragement

▶ Review Week 5 Bible readings and study questions from Mark. Ask if the new believer has any questions. (See Bible Background Information [page 137] for additional helps if needed.)

SHARE TOGETHER

▶ Give the new believer examples of how you have overcome temptation.

▶ Describe examples of things you have struggled with and how God has helped you overcome them.

▶ Discuss the times you have struggled with discouragement and how you overcame it.

▶ Ask the new believer these questions:

 ? How does God help you to see the weak areas in your life?

 ? How can God help you overcome temptation?

 ? When have you felt discouraged?

PRAY TOGETHER

▶ Ask the new believer for any prayer requests.

▶ Pray together.

WRAPPING UP

▶ Schedule your next meeting with the new believer.

▶ Remind the new believer to:
  ▪ Read Week 6 of The New Believer's Handbook,
  ▪ Read the Week 6 Bible readings from Mark, and
  ▪ Complete the study questions.

WEEK 5

HOW CAN I BE A STRONG CHRISTIAN?

As a Christian, you need strength to overcome life's challenges and to serve the Lord effectively. You may feel inadequate on your own, but if you trust in God and not only in yourself, He will help you through any battle.

The first time you're weak and fail you may think, "It's no use. I can't live the Christian life. I might as well give up." The enemy, Satan, puts these thoughts into your mind to discourage you. You may feel defeated when you face temptation to sin—even if you don't sin. Many things in life can make you feel like a weak Christian, but here are some things you can remember to help you grow strong.

TEMPTATION IS NOT SIN

Temptation is only having the desire or pull to do something you know is wrong. Everyone has these feelings at times, but it is important not to give in to them. Jesus was tempted, but He overcame temptation by resisting it and quoting God's Word. Just like Jesus, you have the strength to overcome any temptation that comes your way!

KNOW YOUR WEAK POINTS

As a new Christian, you may still be struggling with life-controlling issues. Perhaps these are things that have a powerful grip on your life—a bad temper, addictions, or some other weakness. Knowing where you are weak will help you know how to pray for God's help. God understands and will help you overcome these challenges as you trust in Him.

COOPERATE WITH GOD

Rely on Jesus to help you overcome struggles. Jesus Christ lives in your heart through His Holy Spirit, who is called "the Comforter," meaning "one called alongside to help." The Holy Spirit will help you grow as a Christian by developing in you the nine fruit of the Spirit (see Galatians 5:22,23) that together are the character of Christ. God's purpose is to make you like Jesus. To help you better understand about the Holy Spirit, underline the things Jesus promised the Holy Spirit would do in John 14 and 16.

Having an obedient attitude to God will help you become a strong Christian. Obey the Lord when you feel Him suggesting something to you by His Holy Spirit. It is easier to be confident in your actions when you do what you believe God has told you. Also, listen to pastors and other mature Christians. They can help as well.

FOCUS ON GOD'S WORD

Memorize portions of the Bible and think about it often. The writer of the Book of Psalms wrote, "I have hidden your word in my heart that I might not sin against you" (Psalm 119:11). Knowing God's Word strengthens us so we can overcome temptation. When you feel tempted, God can help you remember Bible verses you have studied to help you resist the temptation. Here are two good verses to memorize.

"Submit yourselves, then, to God. Resist the devil, and he will flee from you" (James 4:7).

"No temptation has seized you except what is common to man. And God is faithful; he will not let you be tempted beyond what you can bear. But when you are tempted, he will also provide a way out so that you can stand up under it" (1 Corinthians 10:13).

DON'T GET DISCOURAGED

It is up to you to never give up. A baby that is starting to walk often falls, but only learns to walk by getting up and trying again. If you make a mistake and do something you know is wrong, simply come to God as you did the first time, ask Him to forgive you, and go on.

WEEK FIVE • DAY ONE
Bible Reading & Study Questions from Mark 9:1–13

1. Which disciples did Jesus take with Him to the high mountain? (Mark 9:2) **Peter, James, and John**

2. What happened to Jesus' appearance when He was transfigured (transformed or changed)? (Mark 9:3) **His clothes became dazzling white, whiter than anyone in the world could bleach them.**

3. What two people came and talked with Jesus during His transfiguration? (Mark 9:4) **Elijah and Moses**

4. What did God say about Jesus during the Transfiguration? (Mark 9:7) **"This is my Son, whom I love. Listen to him!"**

WEEK FIVE • DAY TWO
Bible Reading & Study Questions from Mark 9:14–32

1. What did Jesus say is possible for those who believe? (Mark 9:23) **Everything**

2. What response did the father of the demon-possessed boy give to Jesus' statement? (Mark 9:24) **"I do believe; help me overcome my unbelief!"**

3. What did Jesus say was the reason the disciples had not been able to drive out the demon? (Mark 9:29) *"This kind can come out only by prayer."*

4. What teaching of Jesus did the disciples not understand? (Mark 9:31) *"The Son of Man is going to be betrayed into the hands of men. They will kill him, and after three days he will rise."*

WEEK FIVE ▪ DAY THREE
Bible Reading & Study Questions from Mark 9:33–50

1. What were the disciples arguing about? (Mark 9:34) *Who was the greatest*

2. What was Jesus' response? (Mark 9:35) *"If anyone wants to be first, he must be the very last, and the servant of all."*

3. Jesus used an illustration to help us understand the importance of eliminating things from our life that cause us to sin. What three things did Jesus use to describe the things we do, the places we go, and the things we see? (Mark 9:43–48) *Hand, foot, and eye*

WEEK FIVE ▪ DAY FOUR
Bible Reading & Study Questions from Mark 10:1–16

1. Why did the Pharisees ask Jesus about divorce? (Mark 10:2) *To test Him*

2. Why did Jesus say divorce was allowed in the Old Testament law written by Moses? (Mark 10:5) *Because their hearts were hard*

3. How should we come to Jesus? (Mark 10:15) *Like a child*

WEEK FIVE ▪ DAY FIVE
Bible Reading & Study Questions from Mark 10:17–31

1. How did Jesus feel about the rich man? (Mark 10:21) *He loved him.*

2. What did Jesus say people would receive who leave behind family and possessions in exchange for Him and the gospel? (Mark 10:30) *A hundred times as much in this age and eternal life in the age to come*

WEEK FIVE ▪ DAY SIX
Bible Reading & Study Questions from Mark 10:32–45

1. What did Jesus say would happen to Him in Jerusalem? (Mark 10:33–34) *He would be betrayed to the chief priests and teachers of the law. They would condemn Him to death and hand Him over to the Gentiles, who would*

*mock Him and spit on Him, flog Him and kill
Him. Three days later He would rise.*

2. What did Jesus say a person must do to become
great? (Mark 10:43) *Be a servant.*

3. What did Jesus say He ("the Son of Man") came
to earth to do? (Mark 10:45) *To serve, and give
His life as a ransom for many*

WEEK FIVE · DAY SEVEN
Bible Reading & Study Questions from Mark 10:46–52

1. What did blind Bartimaeus shout as Jesus
passed by? (Mark 10:47) *"Jesus, Son of David,
have mercy on me!"*

2. What did Bartimaeus do as soon as Jesus sent
for him? (Mark 10:50) *He threw his cloak aside,
jumped to his feet, and went to Jesus.*

3. When Jesus healed Bartimaeus, what reason
did Jesus give for healing him? (Mark 10:52)
Bartimaeus's faith

4. What did Bartimaeus do after he was healed?
(Mark 10:52) *Followed Jesus*

WHAT DOES GOD EXPECT OF ME?

BEFORE YOU MEET

☐ Schedule a time to meet with the new believer.

☐ Read Week 6 of *The New Believer's Handbook*.

☐ Read the Week 6 Bible readings from Mark.

☐ Review the study questions.

☐ Prepare your testimony of how you have made Christ the Master of your life and have given Him first place.

☐ Think of ways that church involvement has helped you.

MEET TOGETHER

▶ Greet the new believer.

▶ Pray together that God will guide your time of study and fellowship.

REVIEW TOGETHER

▶ Answer the new believer's questions about the Week 6 reading.

▶ Highlight the following from Week 6 in *The New Believer's Handbook* and supporting information:

Spiritual Responsibilities for a Christian:
- Make Christ your Master
- Put Christ first in your life
- Become involved in a church
- Give Christ your time
- Give Christ your abilities
- Give Christ your material possessions
- Tell others of your faith

▶ Review Week 6 Bible readings and study questions from Mark.

Ask if the new believer has any questions. (See Bible Background Information [page 138] for additional helps if needed.)

··········· SHARE TOGETHER

▶ Share with the new believer examples of how you have made Christ the Master of your life and have given Him first place in your life.

▶ Describe ways that church involvement has helped you.

▶ Ask the new believer these questions:

?　How can you give control to Christ so that He is Master of your life?

?　What are some practical ways you can put Jesus first in your life?

?　What have you found easiest about giving Christ your time? What has been the most difficult?

?　What talents and abilities do you have that you can use in service to Christ?

·········· PRAY TOGETHER

▶ Ask the new believer for any prayer requests.
▶ Pray together.

·········· WRAPPING UP

▶ Schedule your next meeting with the new believer.

▶ Remind the new believer to:

▪ Read Week 7 of *The New Believer's Handbook*,
▪ Read the Week 7 Bible readings from Mark, and
▪ Complete the study questions.

WEEK 6

WHAT DOES GOD EXPECT OF ME?

In John 16:13, it says that the Holy Spirit "will guide you into all truth." This truth includes Christian responsibilities. It's all part of growing up spiritually. In the natural, parents give their young children few responsibilities. As the child grows, more responsibilities are given. Let's talk about some spiritual responsibilities.

MAKE CHRIST THE MASTER

To express their loyalty to Jesus when He was living on earth, His disciples often called Him "Lord" or "Master." Jesus accepted this position and said, "If you love me, you will obey what I command" (John 14:15).

As a believer, you now belong to Christ because He bought you by paying for your sins when He died. Obedience shouldn't only be an obligation though. When you think about how much Jesus has done for you by dying for you and saving you from spending eternity in hell, you should be glad to show your love for Him by obeying Him.

PUT CHRIST FIRST IN YOUR LIFE

You make Jesus first in your life through developing your relationship with Him. Develop your relationship by talking to Him and listening to Him. Talk with Him through prayer—at regular times and during the day. Listen to Him through reading the Bible. Think of what you are reading as Jesus' message to you. Make Jesus the center of your life by revolving every activity in your day around how you think Jesus would act and react in the same situation.

BECOME INVOLVED IN A CHURCH

You're part of a new family—the people of God. Show that you belong to the family by being involved in a Bible-believing church. This will give you an increased sense of belonging and will provide an opportunity to help others. Being part of a church and its ministries will minister to your needs as well.

GIVE CHRIST YOUR TIME

To mature as a Christian, it is vital to give Jesus some of your time every day. You should give Him practical time in which you attend church, are involved in church activities, and help other Christians with their needs. You should also give Him personal time to develop your relationship through private devotions (Bible reading, prayer, etc.) and family devotions, if you live with Christian family members. The more time you devote to Jesus, the more you will gain in maturity and spiritual strength!

GIVE CHRIST YOUR ABILITIES

Everyone can do something. If you have special talents or abilities, use them to do the Lord's work. Besides jobs that call for special talents, there are many general tasks you can do. Your pastor and other church leaders will be happy for you to volunteer. Promise the Lord that you will try to do anything you are asked to do for Him.

GIVE CHRIST YOUR MATERIAL POSSESSIONS

Everything you possess is from God, yet He only asks for a small portion back. One important way of giving back to God is through tithing—giving 10 percent of your income to the church. Through tithes, you help support your church and spread the gospel at home and in other nations. Give offerings above your tithe for specific events and occasions. It may sound like a lot, but God will meet and exceed your needs, as you are faithful to Him.

TELL OTHERS OF YOUR FAITH

Christ commanded His disciples to tell others about what He did (Matthew 28:18–20). They told people, who told other people, who told others. The message has passed on like that for almost two thousand years. Eventually someone told you about Jesus Christ, or you would not be a Christian today.

It is now your turn to witness, or tell others about Jesus and what He has done for you. As you witness, it will become easier and more comfortable. Next to your salvation, one of your greatest thrills will be telling someone about Jesus and that person deciding to become a Christian. Make a point to talk to someone about Jesus every day.

WEEK SIX • DAY ONE
Bible Reading & Study Questions from Mark 11:1–11

1. What was special about the colt Jesus sent the disciples to get? (Mark 11:2) *No one had ever ridden it.*

2. What was spread on the road in front of Jesus? (Mark 11:8) *Cloaks and branches*

3. What was shouted as Jesus entered Jerusalem? (Mark 11:9,10) *"Hosanna! Blessed is he who comes in the name of the Lord! Blessed is the coming kingdom of our father David! Hosanna in the highest!"*

WEEK SIX • DAY TWO
Bible Reading & Study Questions from Mark 11:12–19

1. Jesus used the fig tree as an illustration of what was lacking in the religion of His day. What did the fig tree lack? (Mark 11:13) *Fruit*

2. What was the temple supposed to be? (Mark 11:17) *A house of prayer for all nations*

3. What did Jesus say the temple had become?
(Mark 11:17) ***A den of robbers***

4. What did the religious leaders begin to do after
Jesus made the statement? (Mark 11:18) **Look
for a way to kill Him**

WEEK SIX ▪ DAY THREE
Bible Reading & Study Questions from Mark 11:20–33

1. What did Jesus say we must do for our prayers to
be answered? (Mark 11:22,24) **Have faith in God
and believe that you will receive the things you
pray for.**

2. What did Jesus say we must do when we pray
so our Heavenly Father will forgive our sins?
(Mark 11:25) **If you hold anything against
anyone, forgive him.**

3. Why did the religious leaders not want to answer
Jesus' question? (Mark 11:32) **They feared the
people.**

WEEK SIX ▪ DAY FOUR
Bible Reading & Study Questions from Mark 12:1–12

1. In this parable, what did the owner of the
vineyard want to happen when he sent his son
to the tenants? (Mark 12:6) **That the son would
be respected**

2. What did the tenants hope to accomplish by killing the son? (Mark 12:7) **To get the inheritance for themselves**

3. Jesus told this parable to the religious leaders of His day. The vineyard owner represents God, the servants sent to collect the fruit represent the Old Testament prophets, the son represents Jesus, and the "others" represent all who will accept Jesus as Savior. Who do the tenants represent? (Mark 12:12) **The religious leaders**

WEEK SIX ▪ DAY FIVE
Bible Reading & Study Questions from Mark 12:13–17

1. Trying to flatter Jesus, the religious leaders made some key observations about Him. What were their observations? (Mark 12:14) **Jesus was a man of integrity, was not swayed by men, did not show partiality, and taught the way of God in accordance with the truth.**

2. What did the religious leaders ask Jesus to trick Him so that the Roman government would have grounds to arrest Him? (Mark 12:14,15) **"Is it right to pay taxes to Caesar or not? Should we pay or shouldn't we?"**

3. What did Jesus perceive about the religious leaders? (Mark 12:15) **Their hypocrisy and attempt to trap Him**

4. What was their reaction to Jesus' answer?
(Mark 12:17) **They were amazed at Him.**

WEEK SIX • DAY SIX
Bible Reading & Study Questions from Mark 12:18–34

1. What was the Sadducees' question? (Mark 12:23)
**"At the resurrection whose wife will she be,
since the seven were married to her?"**

2. Before we can understand Jesus' response to the
Sadducees, what should we know about their
beliefs? (Mark 12:18) **They did not believe in the
resurrection.**

3. Why did Jesus say the Sadducees were in error
for not believing in the resurrection (eternal life
in heaven)? (Mark 12:24) **They did not know the
Scriptures or the power of God.**

4. What did Jesus say are the two greatest
commandments? (Mark 12:30,31) **"Love the Lord
your God with all your heart and with all your
soul and with all your mind and with all your
strength." "Love your neighbor as yourself."**

WEEK SIX • DAY SEVEN
Bible Reading & Study Questions from Mark 12:35–44

1. What was the crowd's reaction to Jesus' teaching? (Mark 12:37) **They listened to Him with delight.**

2. What will happen to people who only practice an outward religion? (Mark 12:40) **They will be punished severely.**

3. Why did Jesus say the poor widow had given more than all the others at the temple? (Mark 12:44) **"They all gave out of their wealth; but she, out of her poverty, put in everything— all she had to live on."**

HOW CAN I KNOW THE WILL OF GOD?

BEFORE YOU MEET

- ☐ Schedule a time to meet with the new believer.
- ☐ Read Week 7 of *The New Believer's Handbook*.
- ☐ Read the Week 7 Bible readings from Mark.
- ☐ Review the study questions.
- ☐ Prepare to share your testimony with the new believer about your experiences when love for God enabled you to be in His will.
- ☐ Think of ways you have learned to love difficult people.
- ☐ Write down your method for determining God's will.

MEET TOGETHER

- ▶ Greet the new believer.

- ▶ Pray together that God will guide your time of study and fellowship.

REVIEW TOGETHER

- ▶ Answer the new believer's questions about the Week 7 reading.

- ▶ Highlight the following from Week 7 in *The New Believer's Handbook* and supporting information:

    Christians Are to Show Love to God
    - Bring glory to God by your actions
    - Be guided by your love for Jesus
    - Ask, "What can I do that would best please Jesus?"

Christians Are to Show Love to Others (The Golden Rule)

- God's gift of love makes it possible to love difficult people
- Love makes you more considerate to others resulting in a positive witness for Christ

How to Make the Best Choice from Multiple Good Options

- Be patient
- Seek others' advice
- Commit the matter to the Lord

▶ Review Week 7 Bible readings and study questions from Mark. Ask if the new believer has any questions. (See Bible Background Information [page 140] for additional helps if needed.)

·········· SHARE TOGETHER

▶ Share with the new believer instances when love for God has enabled you to be in His will.

▶ Describe examples of how you have learned to love difficult people.

▶ Explain your method of determining God's will from several choices.

▶ Ask the new believer these questions:

  ? How has your love for God guided you over the last seven weeks?

  ? How has your love for others helped you be a witness to them?

  ? What role has love played in making your choices easier or harder?

PRAY TOGETHER

▶ Ask the new believer for any prayer requests.

▶ Pray together.

WRAPPING UP

▶ Schedule your next meeting with the new believer.

▶ Remind the new believer to:
- Read Week 8 of *The New Believer's Handbook*,
- Read the Week 8 Bible readings from Mark, and
- Complete the study questions.

HOW CAN I KNOW THE WILL OF GOD?

How to know the will of God—that's a big enough subject to write volumes on. Yet it is something important for every Christian to know and pursue. After all, since Christ is now your Master and you want to obey Him, you must learn what He wants you to do with your life.

WHEN IT'S A MATTER OF CONDUCT

Everyone knows there is a difference between right and wrong, even people who have never heard of God's law or read the Bible. Jesus taught that the two most important commandments are to love God and to love our neighbor the way we love ourselves (Mark 12:28–31). The second of these commandments means that we should act toward others as we want them to act toward us. This law has become known as "the Golden Rule." Obedience to these two laws is the first step of living in God's will.

You are now Jesus' representative in the world. In deciding how you should live, be guided by your love for Jesus. That love will lead you to a life that glorifies God. When you have an important decision to make, ask yourself, "What can I do that would best please Jesus?" If that is the ruling question in your decisions, you will make the right choice.

WHEN YOU MUST DECIDE WHICH WAY TO GO

Sometimes we must choose how to act from among several options—all of which could please God. How can you decide which is best?

Be patient. Learn to wait on God until He indicates His will to you. Time has a way of working things out. Don't be in a hurry.

Seek the advice of others. Don't be a loner. Let your pastor or another mature Christian help you. Be sure it is someone who will keep your confidence. Someone who is not directly involved in your situation can often see things more clearly than you can.

Commit the matter to the Lord. A famous Christian, George Müller, used this method: He would list the reasons for and against a certain course of action and prayerfully consider the matter for a time. Then he would decide to move in a certain direction. He would remove from his mind as much of his own desires as possible, and then ask God to block his path if it were not His will. Over a period of fifty years Müller found this approach successful.

GETTING ALONG WITH OTHERS

It is God's will that you treat everyone in love, whether it is easy or not. If you haven't learned this yet, you will soon discover that no one is perfect and even Christians can be hard to get along with sometimes. Just like you, God is trying to work in their lives to make them more like Jesus.

You will naturally be drawn to make certain Christians close friends. Other Christians may be a challenge to be friendly with. Remember that we all have traits that others may find annoying, but God wants all Christians to treat each other like brothers and sisters in a loving family.

The most important gift you can ask for from God is the ability to love Him and others at all times. This love is vital because it causes you to develop all the traits God wants you to have. Love will make you want a close relationship with God. Love will make you considerate of others. Love will make you want to witness to others. Love can even help you accept those who seem impossible.

WEEK SEVEN ▪ DAY ONE
Bible Reading & Study Questions from Mark 13:1–23

1. What did Jesus say about the stones of the temple? (Mark 13:2) ***"Not one stone here will be left on another; every one will be thrown down."***

2. List four end-time signs that Jesus described as the "beginning of birth pains." (Mark 13:5–8) *False messiahs, wars and rumors of wars, earthquakes, and famines*

3. What will happen to one who "stands firm till the end" in the time of persecution? (Mark 13:13) *They will be saved.*

4. What does Jesus tell us to do in response to His warnings about the end-time? (Mark 13:23) *Be on guard.*

WEEK SEVEN ▪ DAY TWO
Bible Reading & Study Questions from Mark 13:24–37

1. What will happen when we see Jesus coming in the clouds? (Mark 13:27) *"He will send his angels and gather his elect from the four winds, from the ends of the earth to the ends of the heavens."*

2. What will never pass away? (Mark 13:31) *Jesus' words*

3. Who knows the day and hour of Christ's return? (Mark 13:32) *Only God, the Father*

4. What does Jesus tell us to do to prepare for His return? (Mark 13:33,37) *Be on guard, be alert, and watch!*

WEEK SEVEN ▪ DAY THREE
Bible Reading & Study Questions from Mark 14:1–11

1. What did the woman do with the alabaster jar filled with expensive perfume? (Mark 14:3) **She broke the jar and poured the perfume on Jesus' head.**

2. What was the reaction of the people who saw her do this? (Mark 14:5) **They were indignant and rebuked her harshly.**

3. What did Jesus say was the purpose of her action? (Mark 14:8) **To prepare His body for burial**

4. What did Judas Iscariot do after this event? (Mark 14:10,11) **He talked to the religious leaders about betraying Jesus and began looking for an opportunity to betray Him.**

WEEK SEVEN ▪ DAY FOUR
Bible Reading & Study Questions from Mark 14:12–31

1. What did Jesus compare the broken bread to? (Mark 14:22) **His body**

2. What did Jesus compare the cup to? (Mark 14:23,24) **His blood of the covenant**

3. Who is Jesus' blood poured out for? (Mark 14:24) **Many**

4. What was Jesus' prediction about Peter?
(Mark 14:30) *Before the rooster would crow twice that night Peter would disown Jesus three times.*

WEEK SEVEN ▪ DAY FIVE
Bible Reading & Study Questions from Mark 14:32–52

1. What did Jesus say is possible for God to do?
(Mark 14:36) *Everything*

2. Whose will did Jesus pray would be done?
(Mark 14:36) *God's will*

3. Why did Jesus tell Peter that he should continue to watch and pray? (Mark 14:38) *So Peter would not fall into temptation*

4. What happened to Jesus' followers when He was arrested? (Mark 14:50) *They deserted Him and fled.*

WEEK SEVEN ▪ DAY SIX
Bible Reading & Study Questions from Mark 14:53–65

1. Who followed at a distance when Jesus was taken for trial before the religious leaders?
(Mark 14:54) *Peter*

2. What were the religious leaders looking for?
(Mark 14:55) *Evidence against Jesus so that they could put Him to death*

3. What was Jesus' reaction to the false accusations against Him? (Mark 14:61) *He remained silent and gave no answer.*

4. When the high priest asked Jesus if He was the Christ, what did Jesus say? (Mark 14:62) *"I am," said Jesus. "And you will see the Son of Man sitting at the right hand of the Mighty One and coming on the clouds of heaven."*

WEEK SEVEN ▪ DAY SEVEN
Bible Reading & Study Questions from Mark 14:66–72

1. How many times did Peter deny knowing Jesus? (Mark 14:68,70,71) *Three times*

2. What happened after Peter's third denial? (Mark 14:72) *The rooster crowed the second time.*

3. What was Peter's reaction as soon as he remembered Jesus' prophecy about his denial? (Mark 14:72) *He broke down and wept.*

WHAT ARE THE TWO BAPTISMS?

BEFORE YOU MEET

☐ Schedule a time to meet with the new believer.

☐ Read Week 8 of *The New Believer's Handbook*.

☐ Read the Week 8 Bible readings from Mark.

☐ Review the study questions.

☐ Prepare to share the testimony of your water baptism and your baptism in the Holy Spirit with the new believer.

MEET TOGETHER

▶ Greet the new believer.

▶ Pray together that God will guide your time of study and fellowship.

REVIEW TOGETHER

▶ Answer the new believer's questions about the Week 8 reading.

▶ Highlight the following from Week 8 in *The New Believer's Handbook* and supporting information:

Water Baptism
- Greek word means to be immersed
- An outward expression of an inward change (salvation)
- Identifies with Christ in His death, burial, and resurrection
- Act of obedience to Christ's command

Holy Spirit Baptism

- Who is the Holy Spirit?
    - Holy Spirit is the Third Person of the Trinity
    - Holy Spirit's role in salvation:
        - Draws us to God
        - Resides in us at the moment of salvation
    - Holy Spirit helps Christians
        - Live a joyful life that pleases God
        - Develop the fruit of the Spirit
        - Be convicted when we sin
        - Overcome temptation
        - Understand, learn, and memorize Scripture
- What is the baptism in the Holy Spirit?
    - Gives greater power for Christian living and witnessing
    - Gift promised by Jesus for all Christians
- How do I receive the baptism in the Holy Spirit?
    - Pray asking God for the gift
    - Speak aloud, praying and praising God
    - Believe that God will give
    - Wait on God's timing
- What is the proof of the baptism in the Holy Spirit?
    - The initial physical evidence of the baptism in the Holy Spirit is speaking in other tongues, a language you do not know
    - Holy Spirit's role in daily Christian life
        - Gives power for witnessing
        - Helps with daily living
        - Provides a Spirit-filled life
        - Pray in tongues in your daily prayer time

NOTE: If the new believer has more questions about the baptism in the Holy Spirit, suggest *The Helper* by Randy Hurst (available from Gospel Publishing House, item 03-7733).

▶ Review Week 8 Bible readings and study questions from Mark. Ask if the new believer has any questions. (See Bible Background Information [page 143] for additional helps if needed.)

SHARE TOGETHER

▶ Share your testimony and include the following
- "When I was baptized in water . . ."
- "When I was baptized in the Holy Spirit . . ."

▶ Ask the new believer these questions:
? When are you available to be baptized in water?
? Have you prayed to be baptized in the Holy Spirit?

PRAY TOGETHER

▶ Pray with the new believer for the baptism in the Holy Spirit (if not already baptized).

▶ Ask the new believer for any prayer requests.

▶ Close in prayer together.

WRAPPING UP

▶ See What Now? (page 122).

WHAT ARE THE TWO BAPTISMS?

By now you probably realize that salvation is just the first step in your spiritual life as a Christian. There are many other important steps you should take. Two of these important steps are the two baptisms.

WATER BAPTISM

One of the most important things you can do in your new life is to follow Jesus' example of water baptism. Water baptism is a way of showing others that you have given your life to Jesus.

The Greek word for baptism is *baptizō*, which means immerse. When you are baptized in water, you will be immersed—put completely under the water. When you go down into the water, it symbolizes Jesus' death and burial, and that your old, sinful life is dead and buried. When you come out of the water, it symbolizes Jesus' resurrection and your new life in Him.

Water baptism is also an act of obedience. After His resurrection, Jesus commanded, "Go and make disciples of all nations, baptizing them in the name of the Father and of the Son and of the Holy Spirit" (Matthew 28:19). As you daily surrender your life to Jesus and become more like Him, He expects that you will obey Him. Water baptism is a first step in being obedient to Jesus.

If you were baptized as a baby, you might wonder if you need to be baptized again. The Bible instructs that water baptism is for anyone who has recognized the need of a Savior, has repented, and believed in Christ (Acts 2:38,41; 8:36–38). Because a baby is unable to repent of sin and accept Christ as Savior, that person should be baptized in water after becoming a Christian.

You should be baptized as soon as possible. Talk to your pastor this week about setting a date and time.

HOLY SPIRIT BAPTISM

To understand the baptism in the Holy Spirit, you need to understand who the Holy Spirit is. He is the Third Person of the Trinity. *Trinity* is a term used to describe the one true and living God, manifested in three Persons: God the Father, God the Son, and God the Holy Spirit. The Father, Son, and Holy Spirit are distinct Persons, and each is God—not three gods, but one God in three Persons.

God the Father is your Creator, maker of the universe, and the giver of all life.

God the Son (Jesus Christ) is your Savior
who became a man to show the world what
God is like. He paid the penalty for your sin and
has provided everlasting life to anyone who will
receive Him.

God the Holy Spirit is your Helper who
assists you in receiving God's forgiveness and
obeying Him. The Holy Spirit also gives you power
to live like Jesus and to tell others about Him.

When you became a Christian, the Holy Spirit
came to live in you. He lives in each Christian to
help that person live a life that pleases God and is
full of joy. The Holy Spirit lets you know when you
sin and gives you power to overcome temptation.
The Holy Spirit also helps you understand,
learn, and remember Scripture. He is your guide,
comforter, helper, and teacher.

Although the Holy Spirit already lives inside you,
the baptism in the Holy Spirit brings His power
in your life to another level. To better understand
the baptism in the Holy Spirit, compare it to water
baptism. Just as water baptism means to be
immersed in water, being baptized in the Holy
Spirit means to be immersed in the Holy Spirit.
The Holy Spirit completely fills you in a greater
way than before.

Before His return to heaven, Jesus said,

> Do not leave Jerusalem, but wait for the gift
> my Father promised, which you have heard
> me speak about. For John baptized with
> water, but in a few days you will be baptized
> with the Holy Spirit. . . . You will receive
> power when the Holy Spirit comes on you;
> and you will be my witnesses in Jerusalem,
> and in all Judea and Samaria, and to the ends
> of the earth (Acts 1:4–5,8).

The next chapter of the Book of Acts records
the coming of this promised gift on the Day of
Pentecost. In your Bible, read Acts 2:1–8, 11–18.

Jesus' closest followers were baptized in the Holy
Spirit and began speaking in languages they had
never learned! We call these other languages
"tongues." Speaking in tongues is the initial
physical evidence, or proof, of being baptized in
the Holy Spirit (Acts 2:4; 10:46; 19:6).

Not only is speaking in tongues part of the initial
experience of being baptized in the Holy Spirit,
it is also a continual part of a Christian's private
prayer life (1 Corinthians 14:2). God directs us to
pray in tongues when we do not know how to
pray for a specific issue. "The Spirit helps us in our
weakness. We do not know what we ought to pray

for, but the Spirit himself intercedes for us with groans that words cannot express" (Romans 8:26).

You need the Holy Spirit's help just as Jesus' first followers did. The Holy Spirit will be your help as He gives you the power and ability to be a witness for Jesus Christ, both in what you do and what you say.

Ask Jesus to baptize you in the Holy Spirit, believe that He will, and wait patiently. It is a gift (Acts 1:4) and a promise: "The promise is for you and your children and for all who are far off—for all whom the Lord our God will call" (Acts 2:39). Ask your pastor or a Christian friend for more information on how to receive this gift from God.

The baptism in the Holy Spirit is not a once-for-all experience. As you continue to stay close to the Lord in prayer and reading His Word, the Holy Spirit will work in you more and more.

WEEK EIGHT • DAY ONE
Bible Reading & Study Questions from Mark 15:1–15

1. Because the religious leaders did not have the authority to sentence Jesus to death they took Him to Pilate, the Roman ruler for that region. What was Pilate's reaction when Jesus gave no response to the false accusations against Him? (Mark 15:5) *He was amazed.*

2. What was the custom at the Feast of Unleavened Bread? (Mark 15:6) *To release a prisoner requested by the people*

3. Why did Pilate offer to release Jesus? (Mark 15:10) *He knew it was out of envy that the chief priests had handed Jesus over to him.*

4. Why did Pilate agree to release Barabbas and have Jesus flogged and crucified? (Mark 15:15) *To satisfy the crowd*

WEEK EIGHT ▪ DAY TWO
Bible Reading & Study Questions from Mark 15:16–20

1. What piece of clothing did the Roman soldiers put on Jesus to mock Him? (Mark 15:17) *A purple robe*

2. What did they place on Jesus' head? (Mark 15:17) *A crown of thorns*

3. What did they call out to Jesus? (Mark 15:18) *"Hail, king of the Jews!"*

4. The soldiers spit on Jesus and struck Him on the head with what? (Mark 15:19) *A staff*

WEEK EIGHT ▪ DAY THREE
Bible Reading & Study Questions from Mark 15:21–32

1. What was Simon from Cyrene forced to do?
   (Mark 15:21) *To carry Jesus' cross*

2. Where was Jesus crucified and what did the
   place's name mean? (Mark 15:22) *Golgotha,
   which means The Place of the Skull*

3. Who was crucified with Jesus? (Mark 15:27) *Two
   robbers, one on Jesus' right and one on His left*

4. Name three groups of people who insulted or
   mocked Jesus as He hung on the cross.
   (Mark 15:29,31,32) *Those who passed by, chief
   priests and teachers of the Law, and those who
   crucified Him*

WEEK EIGHT ▪ DAY FOUR
Bible Reading & Study Questions from Mark 15:33–41

1. What happened from the sixth hour until the ninth
   hour on the day Jesus was crucified? (Mark 15:33)
   Darkness came over the whole land.

2. What did Jesus cry out at the ninth hour?
   (Mark 15:34) *"Eloi, Eloi, lama sabachthani?"—
   which means, "My God, my God, why have you
   forsaken me?"*

3. What happened immediately after Jesus died?
(Mark 15:38) *The curtain of the temple was torn in two from top to bottom.*

4. What was the reaction of the centurion, the Roman solider who oversaw Jesus' crucifixion, after Jesus died? (Mark 15:39) *He said, "Surely this man was the Son of God!"*

WEEK EIGHT ▪ DAY FIVE
Bible Reading & Study Questions from Mark 15:42–47

1. Who requested Jesus' body to prepare it for burial? (Mark 15:43) *Joseph of Arimathea, a prominent member of the Council*

2. Who verified for Pilate that Jesus had already died? (Mark 15:45) *The centurion*

3. List the steps Joseph took to bury Jesus. (Mark 15:46) *Joseph bought some linen cloth, took down the body, wrapped it in the linen, placed it in a tomb cut out of rock, and rolled a stone against the entrance of the tomb.*

WEEK EIGHT ▪ DAY SIX
Bible Reading & Study Questions from Mark 16:1–8

1. What were the women wondering on their way to the tomb early on Sunday morning? (Mark 16:2,3) *"Who will roll the stone away from the entrance of the tomb?"*

2. What did they see when they got there? (Mark 16:4) *The stone had already been rolled away.*

3. Describe the angel that the women saw when they entered the tomb. (Mark 16:5) *A young man dressed in a white robe sitting on the right side of the tomb*

4. What did the angel say to them? (Mark 16:6,7) *"Don't be alarmed," he said. "You are looking for Jesus the Nazarene, who was crucified. He has risen! He is not here. See the place where they laid him. But go, tell his disciples and Peter, 'He is going ahead of you into Galilee. There you will see him, just as he told you.' "*

WEEK EIGHT · DAY SEVEN
Bible Reading & Study Questions from Mark 16:9–20

1. List three people or groups of people Jesus appeared to following His resurrection. (Mark 16:9,12,14) *Mary Magdalene, two while they were walking in the country, and the Eleven*

2. What did Jesus command His followers to do? (Mark 16:15) *Go into all the world and preach the good news to all people.*

3. What will happen to the people who believe the good news and are baptized? (Mark 16:16) *They will be saved.*

4. What will happen to the people who do not believe the good news? (Mark 16:16) **They will be condemned.**

5. What did Jesus' disciples do after Jesus was taken up into heaven? (Mark 16:20) **They went out and preached everywhere.**

6. Who worked with Jesus' followers when they preached and how was the message proven? (Mark 16:20) **The Lord worked with them and signs accompanied the message.**

WHAT NOW?

Now that you've completed your eight-week journey with the new believer, confirm that your friendship will remain even though you may not be meeting weekly.

Remind the new believer that spiritual growth is enhanced by following these spiritual disciplines:

- Bible reading
- Prayer
- Faithful church attendance and involvement

Encourage the new believer to be baptized in water and to pray for the gift of the baptism in the Holy Spirit. Affirm that when they fail, God does not give up on them but is ready to forgive and help them.

WHAT NOW?

Well, the first eight weeks are over. How did you do? Now, what about the future? Let's reemphasize some points and consider a few reminders and tips.

BIBLE READING

Read the Bible every day for at least fifteen minutes. Read the Gospel of Mark through two more times, then start at Matthew and read through the Book of Acts. Move to the first book in the Bible, Genesis, and read it next. Go back and read the New Testament all the way through. Then ask your pastor for a daily Bible reading plan.

As you continue to grow as a Christian, daily Bible reading is one of the most important steps you can take.

PRAYER

Prayer is the lifeline of your spiritual life. Think of God as a best friend you can confide in. Talk to Him daily about your victories as well as your needs.

FIND A CHURCH HOME

Become involved in a good church, attend regularly, and help in every way possible.

BE BAPTIZED IN WATER

The Lord has commanded water baptism. It is one of the ways you can give a public testimony of your salvation and relationship with Jesus.

THE BAPTISM IN THE HOLY SPIRIT

Actively pray to be baptized in the Holy Spirit. He is your Counselor and Friend who is there to help you.

BECOME A GIVER

Give ten cents out of every dollar you earn to the church you have made your church home. This is known as the tithe. Then give offerings as the Lord blesses you and impresses on your heart to give above your tithe.

WHEN YOU FAIL

When you fail, ask God for forgiveness, just as you did the first time. He will never give up on you. But determine by His help not to fail in the same way again.

WHAT NOW?

It depends on you. By following these suggestions, you will begin to grow as a Christian and mature spiritually.

PATTERN FOR BIBLE STUDY

When you study the Bible, use the following questions to help you.

INTENT
What does this passage say and really mean?

DIFFICULTY
What does it say that I don't understand?

COMPARISON
What similar thoughts are found elsewhere in the Bible?

PROMISES
What blessings are stated that are for all believers?

WARNINGS
What warnings apply to my everyday life?

COMMANDS
What commands should I obey?

WEEKLY PRAYER GUIDE

Make it a habit to pray every day. Use the following prayer guide as a suggested direction for your daily, dedicated prayer time.

SUNDAY

S is for Sinners; pray especially that God will reach those who don't know Christ through the church services.

MONDAY

M is for Missionaries; pray for those who go to places other than their home to spread the message of Jesus.

TUESDAY

T is for Tasks; pray about your particular work for God.

WEDNESDAY

W is for Workers; pray for the pastor and others who work in your church.

THURSDAY

T is for Thanksgiving; express gratitude for what God has done for you and others.

FRIDAY

F is for Families and Friends; pray for their salvation if they are not saved and that they will continue to grow closer to Christ.

SATURDAY

S is for Saints, fellow believers; pray that they will grow into mature believers.

SUGGESTED MEMORY VERSES (BY TOPIC)

COMMUNION
1 Corinthians 11:26

END-TIME
John 14:2,3
Acts 1:11
1 Corinthians 15:52
1 Thessalonians 4:16,17
Titus 2:13

FAITH
John 20:29
2 Corinthians 5:7
Ephesians 2:8
2 Timothy 1:12
Hebrews 11:1
Hebrews 11:6

GIVING/MONEY
Matthew 6:24
Luke 6:38
2 Corinthians 9:6,7
Philippians 4:11
1 Timothy 6:9,10

GOD
Genesis 1:1
Genesis 1:27
Exodus 20:7
Deuteronomy 6:4

GOD'S WORD
Deuteronomy 6:6–9
Joshua 1:8
Psalm 1:2,3
Psalm 119:11
Psalm 119:105
Matthew 5:17,18
Matthew 24:35
John 1:1
John 15:7
Acts 17:11
Romans 1:16
Romans 10:17
1 Thessalonians 2:13
2 Timothy 2:15
2 Timothy 3:14–17
Hebrews 4:12

GUIDANCE
Psalm 16:11
Psalm 37:4
Proverbs 3:5,6
Proverbs 16:9

HEALING
Isaiah 53:5
Acts 3:6
James 5:14–16

HOLY LIVING
Deuteronomy 6:25
Psalm 24:3,4
Psalm 119:3
John 14:15
John 15:10
Acts 24:16
Philippians 1:9–11
Philippians 2:3
Philippians 4:9
Colossians 3:9,10
1 Thessalonians 5:23
Hebrews 12:14
1 Peter 1:15,16

HOLY SPIRIT
Acts 1:4,5
Acts 1:8
Acts 2:4
Acts 2:38,39
Acts 4:31
Galatians 5:22,23

JESUS CHRIST
Matthew 1:23
Matthew 16:16
Matthew 28:6
Luke 1:35
Luke 3:22
John 1:3
2 Corinthians 5:21
Philippians 2:9–11
Hebrews 7:23–28
Hebrews 13:8
1 Peter 2:22
Revelation 22:13

LOVE
Matthew 5:44
Luke 10:27
John 13:35
John 15:13
1 Corinthians 13
Ephesians 3:17–19
Hebrews 10:24
1 John 4:8
1 John 4:20

MINISTRY
Matthew 5:16
Mark 16:15
Hebrews 10:25
1 Peter 3:15
1 Peter 4:10

PEACE

Psalm 4:8
John 14:27
John 16:33
Romans 5:1
Philippians 4:7

PRAYER

Matthew 6:9–13
Matthew 21:22
1 Thessalonians 5:17

SALVATION

Proverbs 28:13
Luke 19:10
John 1:11,12
John 1:29
John 3:3
John 3:16,17
John 6:35
John 10:10
John 11:25
John 14:6
John 20:31
Acts 4:12
Acts 16:31
Romans 1:16
Romans 5:8
Romans 6:23
Romans 10:9
Romans 12:1,2
2 Corinthians 5:17
Galatians 2:20
Ephesians 2:8
James 1:22
2 Peter 1:20,21
1 John 1:9
1 John 4:9
Revelation 1:3

TEMPTATIONS AND TRIALS

Genesis 4:7
Matthew 26:41
1 Corinthians 10:13
Ephesians 6:10–18
James 1:2–4
James 1:12

THANKFULNESS

Psalm 136:1
Colossians 3:17
1 Thessalonians 5:18

WATER BAPTISM

Matthew 28:19
Romans 6:4

BIBLE BACKGROUND INFORMATION

Bible Background Information is in the order the topics are covered in the Scripture passage.

MARK 1 & 2

Holy Spirit

This topic is covered in more detail in Week 8 of *The New Believer's Handbook* but the new believer may have questions from this passage.

- The Holy Spirit is God.
- He is the Third Person of the Trinity:
  - God the Father
  - God the Son
  - God the Holy Spirit
- God in all three Persons was present at Jesus' water baptism.

Demon possession

- An evil spirit enters a nonbeliever and takes control.
- The New Testament gives examples of demon possession causing illness in some cases as well as wild behavior.
- The demon's main goal is to destroy the possessed person.
- Jesus proved in His earthly ministry that He has power over demons and Satan. "The one [Jesus] who is in you is greater than the one [Satan] who is in the world" (1 John 4:4).
- A Christian cannot be demon possessed.

Sabbath

- Day of worship and rest
- According to the law of Moses, no work could be done on the Sabbath.
- The Jewish religious leaders created additional strict rules about what was considered work on the Sabbath.

- Jewish people observe the Sabbath on Saturday (sundown Friday to sundown Saturday).
- Christians observe the Sabbath on Sunday because it was the day of Jesus' resurrection.
- The Christian's primary focus for the Sabbath is that it is a day for worship and church attendance.

Synagogue

Jewish house of worship

Leprosy

- Contagious skin disease
- People with leprosy were considered unclean by the Jewish people. This meant that people with leprosy:
  - were social outcasts
  - could not participate in religious ceremonies
  - had to live apart from the main community
  - could not be touched by anyone
  - had to proclaim loudly that they were unclean whenever they approached anyone
  - had to show themselves to a priest to be declared clean if they believed they were healed of leprosy

Groups of religious leaders in the New Testament

- Teachers of the Law or Scribes: Well-educated Jewish men who studied the Old Testament Law and Scriptures and worked as copyists, editors, and teachers.
- Pharisees: Religious and political leaders who had very strict rules in addition to the Old Testament Law. They were adamant about observing those rules and disapproved of anyone who did not keep them. Generally, their observance of rules was outward instead of inward; their hearts were far from God. The Pharisees believed in miracles and the resurrection of the dead (life after death and heaven). The Pharisees served as teachers of the Law or scribes and as members of the Sanhedrin, the Jewish highest court. Many Pharisees opposed Jesus.

- Sadducees: Religious leaders who did not believe in miracles, the resurrection of the dead, or heaven and hell. They served as teachers of the Law or scribes, chief priests, and as members of the Sanhedrin. The Sadducees also opposed Jesus.

Tax collectors

Jews who were hated by other Jewish people because:

- they worked for the hated Roman government and were considered traitors

- they often cheated people by charging more taxes than required, keeping the extra for themselves

Fasting

Doing without food and using that time to pray. Many people used fasting as an opportunity to show their spirituality rather than out of a sincere desire to pray.

David

One of the main Old Testament Jewish kings

Son of Man

Jesus often used this title to refer to himself.

- The title literally means The Man.

- The expression refers to Old Testament prophecy and is another way of saying Son of God.

- Jesus was fully God and fully man.

Jesus' identity

Jesus often told people not to tell others who He was or what He had done for them because it wasn't time yet for everyone to know. God had a plan in mind, and the timing was in His hands.

Blasphemy

Cursing God or showing contempt or a lack of respect for Him

Blasphemy against the Holy Spirit

- Person willfully attributes the work of the Holy Spirit to Satan.
- It is a result of a hardened heart.
- It is not a onetime occurrence, but the result of repeated and purposeful sin.
- This sin cannot be forgiven because when people allow themselves to reach this point, they no longer desire forgiveness. Anyone who fears that they have committed this sin can know they have not.

Parables

Jesus often taught using parables, stories about familiar things with a spiritual meaning.

MARK 5 & 6

Pigs

According to the law of Moses, pigs are unclean animals—not to be eaten or even touched. The story of the pigs in chapter 5 shows that Jesus was in a Gentile (non-Jewish) location at this time. Jesus may have allowed the demons to enter the pigs as tangible evidence that they had left the man.

Feeding the five thousand

The Bible does not include the number of women and children who were present when Jesus multiplied the bread and fish and fed five thousand men. The total number of people present may have been as many as ten thousand.

MARK 7 & 8

Clean or Unclean

Jewish law specified certain behaviors and foods as unclean or defiled. The Pharisees used outward ceremonial acts of cleansing for unclean behaviors. Jewish people avoided unclean food altogether. These outward rituals did not clean the impurity of the heart.

Gentiles

Anyone who is not Jewish is a Gentile.

- In New Testament times the Jewish people were very prejudiced toward Gentiles. Any association with a Gentile was believed to make a Jewish person ritually unclean. The Syrophoenician woman was a Gentile.

- Jesus' statement to the woman showed that He came first to the Jewish nation and then to the Gentiles. It was not meant as a derogatory statement toward the woman.

- Jesus helped another Gentile when He healed the demon possessed man (Mark 5).

- Jesus ministered to both Jews and Gentiles throughout His earthly ministry.

Feeding the four thousand

The record of this miraculous feeding also includes only the count of the men present. By adding in an estimate of the women and children present, Jesus must have fed between six and eight thousand people that day.

Yeast

Yeast (leaven) often symbolizes evil or sin in the Bible.

The Messiah/Christ

- The Hebrew term *Messiah* means *Anointed One*. In the Old Testament the word *anointed* described a special king who was enabled by God to deliver his people and establish God's kingdom.

- In Greek the word for Messiah is *Christos* from which we get the English word *Christ*.

- In New Testament times the Jewish people mistakenly thought the Messiah would be a political deliverer, setting the Jewish people free from rule by the Roman government, establishing his kingdom, and ruling as king. Many Jewish people had a difficult time accepting Jesus as the Messiah because He did not fit their definition.

- Christians understand that as Messiah, Jesus is our spiritual deliverer, setting us free from sin and death.

- The Jewish people did not understand that the first stage of the Messiah's mission would be to suffer, be rejected, and to die for the sins of all mankind. The second stage of Christ's mission will be completed at Jesus' Second Coming when He will set up His kingdom on earth.

Crucifixion

A humiliating and extremely painful form of execution. For a disciple to "take up his cross" and follow Jesus meant that the believer must be willing to suffer humiliation and death for Jesus.

MARK 9 & 10

··· Transfiguration

Jesus' physical appearance changed to show His glory as the Son of God.

- Elijah was an Old Testament prophet who worked many miracles. Elijah's presence at Jesus' transfiguration represents Old Testament prophecy.

- Moses was the Old Testament deliverer of God's people from slavery in Egypt. Moses wrote the first five books of the Bible and recorded God's law. Moses' presence at Jesus' transfiguration represents the Old Testament law.

··· Son of David

Title used in New Testament for Jesus

- Jesus was a descendant of King David through both of His parents.
  - Mary's lineage was through the line of David's son Nathan (genealogy found in the Gospel of Luke).
  - Joseph's lineage was through the line of David's son King Solomon (genealogy found in the Gospel of Matthew).
- The Old Testament tells us that the Messiah would be a descendant of King David
- Being a descendant of David validates Jesus' role as Messiah and King.

Triumphal Entry

The Triumphal Entry was a fulfillment of an Old Testament prophecy which revealed that the Messiah would ride into Jerusalem peacefully on a donkey (Zechariah 9:9).

Hosanna

Means *save now*.

Temple

- Located in Jerusalem. Synagogues, Jewish houses of worship, were located in various cities and villages. Sacrifices were made only at the temple.

- David's son, Solomon, built the original temple.

- The original temple was destroyed when the Babylonians invaded Israel and took the Jewish people into captivity during Old Testament times.

- The temple was rebuilt following the Israelites' captivity in Babylon. King Herod refurbished the temple hundreds of years later. It was destroyed again by the Romans during the fall of Jerusalem in AD 70. It will be rebuilt during the end-time.

- In Bible times, the temple was used for:
  - Worship
  - Prayer
  - Teaching and instruction
  - Animal sacrifices
    - In the Old Testament, the only way for sins to be forgiven was through an animal sacrifice.
    - According to the law of Moses, priests were the only ones who could offer the animal sacrifices.
    - Animal sacrifices are no longer necessary because Jesus gave himself as the sacrifice for the forgiveness of all sin.

Animal Sacrifices

Originally, an animal for sacrifice was to come from one's own flock or herd. Due to circumstances of travel, Jewish people in Jesus' day bought the animals when they arrived at the temple. Often, the animals sold at the temple did not meet the qualifications as a perfect sacrifice.

Cleansing of the temple

Jesus' cleansing of the temple was another fulfillment of Messianic prophecy (Malachi 3:1–3). The money changers cheated people by charging a higher exchange rate than was necessary and pocketing the extra.

MARK 13 & 14

End-time events

- Mark 13 records various end-time events. Some events occur only in the end-time, while some have multiple fulfillments:
  - Time between the writing of the Old and New Testaments
  - Persecution of the Early Church
  - Fall of Jerusalem in AD 70
  - Time of warning signs leading to the Rapture
  - End-time

- Events is chapter 13 are interwoven and not necessarily in chronological order. Use this simplified chronological timeline if the new believer has further questions. Emphasize that understanding will result from Bible study and growth as a Christian.
  - Rapture of the Church (the Blessed Hope): Christians, both living and dead, will meet Jesus in the air and receive their new transformed body as Jesus takes us with Him to heaven.
  - Judgment Seat of Christ: Christians will be judged and rewarded in heaven for their life on earth.
  - Marriage Supper of the Lamb: Banquet in heaven that celebrates the wedding of Christ and the Church.
  - The Great Tribulation: Seven-year period takes place on earth immediately following the Rapture while Christians are in heaven. During this time there will be many plagues poured out on the earth as acts of God's judgment. The Antichrist will rule the world.
  - The Abomination (something detestable) that Causes Desolation (devastation)
    - Phrase first appears in the Old Testament Book of Daniel. It referred to an event that occurred during the time between the Old and New Testaments. An invader offered a pig as a sacrifice on the altar in the temple.

- Prophecy was fulfilled a second time when the Romans conquered Jerusalem in AD 70 and desecrated the temple.
  - A final fulfillment will occur when an image of Antichrist will be set up in Jerusalem (see Revelation 13:14,15).
- The Second Coming: Jesus, along with the Christians in heaven, returns to earth at the end of the Great Tribulation. He defeats the Antichrist and Satan, establishes His kingdom on earth, and sets up the Millennial Reign.
- Battle of Armageddon: Conflict between Jesus and the Antichrist and his followers. Antichrist is defeated, he and his false prophet are thrown into the Lake of Fire for all eternity, and Satan is thrown into a bottomless pit for a thousand years.
- Millennial Reign of Christ: Jesus and the Christians rule the earth for a thousand years. There will be peace and safety, and the earth will be restored to perfect order. All nations will be under the rule of Jesus. Those who survived the Tribulation will continue to marry and have children during this time.
- Battle of Gog and Magog: Satan is released from the bottomless pit and recruits followers from those living on earth to form a massive army to rebel against God. Satan and his followers are defeated. Satan is thrown into the Lake of Fire for all eternity.
- Great White Throne Judgment: Those who have died without accepting Jesus as Lord and Savior will be judged and thrown into the Lake of Fire for all eternity.
- Creation of the New Heavens and New Earth: Christians will spend all eternity with God and Jesus.

⋯ Passover and the Feast of Unleavened Bread:

Commemorates the tenth plague on Egypt (death of all firstborn males) that God used to deliver His people from slavery in the Book of Exodus.

- Passover
  - To avoid the tenth plague, God told the Israelites to sacrifice a perfect lamb and spread its blood over the doorposts of their house. When the death angel went through the land and saw the blood, he would pass over that house without killing the firstborn son.

- Jesus is our perfect Passover Lamb. When we accept Christ's sacrifice, God no longer sees our sin, but instead He sees Jesus' blood. We are spared from spiritual death, the result of sin.

- Feast of Unleavened Bread
  - At the first Passover meal, the Israelites ate the Passover lamb and unleavened bread. God directed the Israelites to eat unleavened bread for two reasons:
    - Leaven (yeast) is symbolic of sin and slavery. Eating bread without leaven (unleavened) symbolizes eating bread without sin and bondage.
    - Preparing bread with leaven is time-consuming because the leaven has to rise. The Passover meal was to be eaten quickly because the Israelites were escaping from slavery in Egypt. Preparing the bread without leaven represented the quickness with which they would leave slavery.
  - Jesus is the Unleavened Bread. He is perfect, without sin, and His sacrifice sets us free from the bondage of sin.

Rabbi

Means *teacher*

Sanhedrin

Jewish ruling court, comprised of Pharisees and Sadducees

MARK 15 & 16

Jesus' death

The Jewish people could not sentence a prisoner to death since they were under Roman rule. The Jewish leaders took Jesus to Pilate, the Roman governor, and convinced him to sentence Jesus.

Details of Jesus' arrest, trial, and crucifixion fulfilled Old Testament prophecy.

Curtain of the temple

- Covered the opening to the room in the temple called the Most Holy Place or the Holy of Holies.

- The Most Holy Place represented the very presence of God. Only the high priest could enter the Most Holy Place, once a year on the Day of Atonement when he offered sacrifice for the forgiveness of the people's sins.

- The curtain was very tall and very thick, and could not be ripped or torn easily. That the curtain was ripped from the top down indicates that it was done supernaturally by God.

- The curtain being torn symbolizes that Jesus' death provided direct access to the presence of God and the forgiveness of sins.

Centurion

Roman soldier who commanded about one hundred men

Preparation Day

Jewish law prohibited work on the Sabbath, so they prepared their food and anything needed for the Sabbath day in advance.

Sabbath

The Sabbath was observed from sunset to sunset, i.e., from Friday evening until Saturday evening. Jesus died on a Friday so the Sabbath was quickly approaching.

Preparation for burial

The women did not have time to follow the Jewish customs for preparing Jesus' body for burial because of the approaching Sabbath. Early Sunday morning, they went to His tomb to prepare His body for burial.